AF428315

Mad Dog!
Detroit Tiger Dick McAuliffe

By
Tom McAuliffe

Next Stop Paradise Publishing
Ft. Walton Beach, Florida, USA

Mad Dog!
Detroit Tiger Dick McAuliffe
by Tom McAuliffe

SECOND EDITION - 2023

For more information email:
bookinfo@nextstopparadise.com

WWW.AUTHORTOMMCAULIFFE.COM

Dedication

To my Brother Matt, my Brother in Law
Chris and Brother in Law John who instilled
in me a love of the game and to anyone who
has ever faced down a 100mph Fastball!

100% of the profits of this book will be donated to The Alzheimer's Foundation of America

VERY SPECIAL THANKS TO:
Sports Writers George Cantor,
Peter Zanardi, John Cizik and Karl Ziomek
without whom this book would not
have been possible.

Richard John 'Dick' McAuliffe
November 29, 1939 – May 13, 2016

Table of Contents

Batter Up…………………………………Pg. 3

Forward……………………………………Pg. 9

Chapter 1: Connecticut Tiger..…..Pg. 13

Chapter 2: Mr. Baseball…………Pg. 21

Chapter 3: The '68 Tigers………Pg. 43

Chapter 4: The Hustler…………Pg. 53

Chapter 5: Tiger Stadium………Pg. 63

Chapter 6: Bottom of the 9th……Pg 73

Chapter 7: PAR, Wash & Camp.…Pg 83

Chapter 8: Cooperstown?..……..Pg. 89

Chapter 9: Pics, Clips, Stats…..Pg. 103

Quiz…………………………..……Pg. 109

Resources………………………Pg. 112

Batter Up!

I spent my errant youth at the corner of Michigan and Trumbull Avenues in Detroit. We would spend a fortune to park, walk through iffy neighborhoods and then you would see it. Built in 1924, the blue-grey monstrosity of Tiger Stadium was like a garden of eden for me. After the dullness of the city streets, I remember walking up the ramp and coming out into the sunlight and seeing that emerald diamond of grass for the first time…it was heavenly. Nicknamed "The Corner" it was formerly known as Navin Field, and then later, Briggs Stadium—though it hosted baseball games on the site since 1912. Needless to say, there's some history there. The stadium could hold upwards of 50,000 people and when the Tiger fans roared, you could hear them across the Detroit River in Windsor, Canada! The sound they made was truly thunderous and shook the foundation of the huge stadium.

Together brother-in-law and I conned our way into the second base upper level gate during the sixth inning stretch of game two of the 1984 Tiger dream team ALCS playoffs. Playing off my good Irish heritage I said, "Father Burns at St. Lawrence is inside and we are doing an article for the church paper." I recited a silent prayer as Chris Bockelman rolled his eyes as if to say, "I am not with this guy!" The seats were way up in "Reefer

Row," a section of the bleachers where one can smoke a cannabis joint and not get hassled. But we got in for free and enjoyed the rest of the game. The Tigers won it 3-2 over the Angels. There were lots of fun memories like that at "The Corner."

I can vividly recall the smell of the Coney Island hotdogs, the peanuts and cotton candy, and of course Stroh's Bohemian Beer. Part of it was the exuberance of youth. Looking back now at 65, with those fond memories, I can say that the game of Baseball taught me vital lessons about life. We also always had a hell of a good time! That and the fact that when I could not talk with my Dad or elders about anything, I could always talk with them about our national past time. It was a unifying factor when nothing else was. Add to all that is the fact that Detroit News and Tigers sportswriter George Cantor was one of my professors at Oakland College. He instilled a passion for accuracy, brevity, and most of all… baseball! But I digress.

This book, number four in the five-volume "The McAuliffe Series," is about my distant relative, the Detroit Tiger and World Series Champ Dick McAuliffe. All of the McAuliffe clan traces their roots back to the 1680s in County Cork, Ireland.

With my personal first hand experiences at "The Corner," press clippings of the day, oral history interviews done with Peter Zanardi and John Cizik for the Society for American Baseball Research, and mementos from the McAuliffe family, I am able to document Dick McAuliffe's life. Especially his talents on the diamond, his perseverance, general zest for life, dedication to family, and his deep love of baseball. He was another McAuliffe clan member who excelled and made a significant contribution to our world.

While I never met him one-on-one, he did wave at me at the stadium when I was sitting behind home plate along the 3rd base line in 1970. I had yelled out, "Yo, Cousin Dick!" and he actually acknowledged me with a wave. He always loved the fans. Tiger Stadium was also, in my opinion, the very best place to watch a ball game. The fans can sit closer to the players than at any other park within Major League Baseball (MLB). It was a cathedral; the religion was baseball, and I was a devoted disciple. I followed his career like no other and was proud to share the same last name.

A MLB "All-Star" three years in a row from 1965 to 1967, Dick McAuliffe was the Tigers' "spark plug;" he was a second baseman but also played shortstop and third base. With a reputation for toughness and feistiness on the field, he was awarded the nickname "Mad Dog" for his quick temper. But he also had a lovable, fun-loving side —and the scrappy infielder was very protective of his fellow teammates. Other teams knew that when you played in Tiger Stadium, you didn't cross him

—nor his teammates. There would be some sort of retribution. Every time.

The combative Detroit Tiger, with eyebrows like 60 Minutes' Andy Rooney, had an unorthodox, wide-open left-leg-lifted batting stance. He was always a sight to behold at home plate. With Bat held high, wiggling above his head, he would be leaning back in the box with his front foot up in the air and the bat cocked just so…he would put his whole body into each swing. It's something imitated on every playground both then and now. The only thing better than seeing it all in person would be listening to Ernie Harwell the voice of the Tigers on WRJ-AM…he was a staple and the best "color man" in baseball broadcasting. When I close my eyes, I can still hear him calling a game!

During the 14 seasons the hard-nosed All-Star infielder played for the Tigers, he helped to take them to the 1968 World Series championship and beyond. Like most ballplayers, McAuliffe was seen by management as a commodity and despite his contributions to the ball club he loved since he was 16, he was unceremoniously traded to the Boston Red Socks, where he played two seasons. He then began 1975 as the Manager of Double-A farm team, "The Bristol Red Sox," located in McAuliffe's native state of Connecticut. He eventually retired from professional baseball at the age of 45, coming home to Connecticut in 1976.

A special thanks to Dick's daughter, Mary, and his grandson, JP, who were both very helpful in the creation of this book in providing background and pictures. Mrs. McAuliffe, Dick's wife Joanne, a spry woman in her 70's, was recovering from surgery and would only comment, "They love a ball player…but only when they're winning!" True enough.

McAuliffe's numbers have yet to net him a plaque in Cooperstown, and perhaps never will—but I would submit, as others have, that there is more to a team and to this wonderful game than just numbers and statistics. He was the glue that held the Tigers together! Every team needs a "spark plug"—a player that connects and can rally the other players even when things get tough…a player that's a passionate ignition source making positive things happen on the field and in the clubhouse.

That was Dick "Mad Dog" McAuliffe… and *this* is his inspiring story.

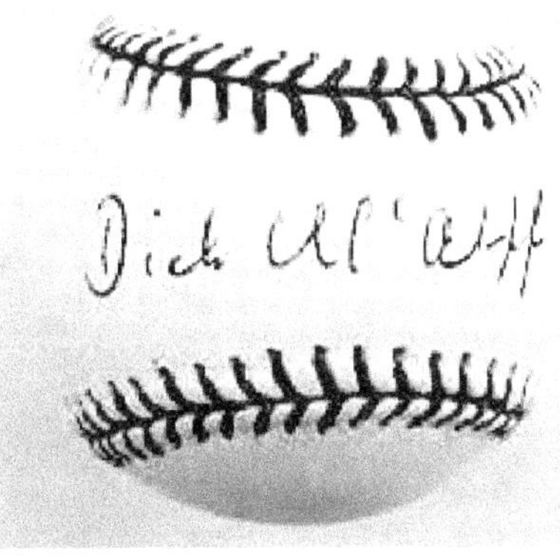

Tom

Fall 2022

FORWARD

The Swinging '60s was a tumultuous decade: the Civil Rights movement, the Vietnam War, the assassinations of President Kennedy, his brother Robert, and the Reverend Martin Luther King Jr.—not to mention an emerging generation gap. Nevertheless, many people around the world still consider the '60s their favorite decade. After all, it gave us The Beatles, a man on the moon and generally was known as an "age for the better," a carefree time of innovation, wonderful music and great Baseball.

It also offered some of the most iconic professional baseball in history. Mickey Mantle (on the East Coast) and Willie Mays (on the West) still dominated the headlines as Major League Baseball expanded west and south. Roger Maris bested Babe Ruth's single-season home run record and the long dominion of "The Damn Yankees" ground to a halt. Sandy Koufax's exploding curveball "fell off a table" and Juan Marichal kicked at the sky before delivering to the plate. The Mets went from feeble to amazin'.

1968 marked the "Year of the Pitcher" with Detroit's Denny McLain winning 31 games (a first since Dizzy Dean in 1934) and St. Louis's Bob Gibson recording a microscopic 1.12 Earned Run Average – the lowest ERA in over a century. Gibson pitched over 300 innings and recorded 13

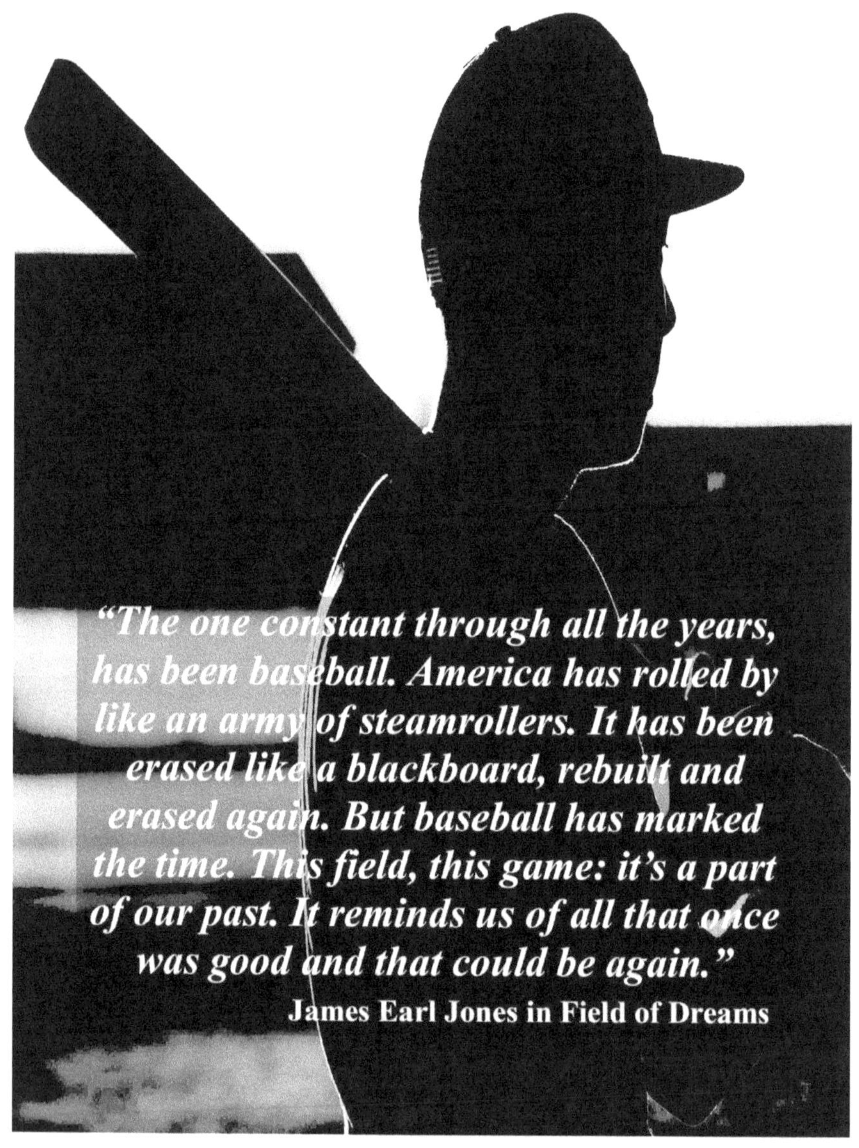

"The one constant through all the years, has been baseball. America has rolled by like an army of steamrollers. It has been erased like a blackboard, rebuilt and erased again. But baseball has marked the time. This field, this game: it's a part of our past. It reminds us of all that once was good and that could be again."
James Earl Jones in Field of Dreams

shutouts. McLain threw 336 innings and started 41 times. Pitching was so overwhelming that the overall batting average sank to .237. Great pitching caused so much concern that the mound was lowered after the season and the strike zone started to shrink. It got harder to get a hit!

That season also gave baseball fans their last "true champion," the come-from-behind, never-say-die Detroit Tigers, who captured their first American League pennant since 1945 and then proceeded to rally from a three-games-one deficit in the World Series to upset the heavily favored Cardinals in seven games. That was the final season that the winners of the American and National leagues went directly to the World Series. The format expanded to divisional play the following season and eventually added wild-card teams to the three and five-game series of MLB's postseason format.

For natives of the Detroit area, 1968 remains hallowed ground. The 1968 Tigers were not only a championship team, they were also in many ways a welcome bridge from hell to heaven. In 1967, some of the most destructive and violent American race rioting occurred in the Motor City. Of the civilians, police officers, firefighters, and National Guardsmen directly involved, 45 were killed and nearly 500 were wounded as the looting, arson, and chaos spread throughout the community. No one was immune—not even the MLB team.

An integral part of this team's story during the 1960s was the player named Dick "Mad Dog" McAuliffe who grew up on the East Coast and would remain in the Tiger lineup for 14 seasons; he proved to be pivotal during the epic 1968 season. A perfect fit, he was the right player for just the right team at just the right moment in time.

In '*Mad Dog! Detroit Tiger Dick McAuliffe*', distant relative, Detroit native, and award-winning author Tom McAuliffe enthusiastically tells his inspirational story. After all, you never cheer quite as hard for a team like the one you cheered for when you were 12!

Karl Ziomek is the former president of the Michigan Press Association and served as a local sports editor and managing editor of newspapers in the Detroit area for decades. In 2018 to celebrate the 50th anniversary of the '68 title, he wrote a game-by-game account of the Tigers' championship season that is still enjoyed by fans on Facebook (including the author, who met Ziomek online last summer).

*"There are only two seasons:
Winter… and Baseball."*
Sportswriter Bill Veeck, Jr.

CHAPTER 1

Connecticut Tiger

*"You train kids in their early years and
you can do anything you want with that child."*
Manager Sparky Anderson
(on why he prefers younger ballplayers)

*"If you're not practicing, somebody else is,
somewhere, and he'll be ready to take your job."*
Player Brooks Robinson

Richard John "Dick" McAuliffe grew up in a Norman Rockwell painting of small town America. Born November 29, 1939 in Hartford, Connecticut to an Italian mother and an Irish father, he was the typical boy next door with a passion for sports. His parents, Bill and Mary Rose McAuliffe, had five children; there was their son, Richard (Dick), his brothers George and William, and his sisters Eleanor and Mary. Together they grew up in the tiny town of Unionville, which was " not exactly a breeding spot for major league athletes," according to Sports Columnist Jim Murray, another Connecticut native. "Chickens are more along its line…Unionville has about nine months of winter," Murray recalled. "And summer is apt to be three months of thunder showers." It is a small community and school sports was central to its interest and existence. Still is.

He was a natural athlete and a born ball player. Dick showed his athletic prowess early on playing in his local little league. He attended Farmington High School in Connecticut, where he made his initial impact on the baseball diamond. At 5-feet-10 and only 140 pounds, Dick was not big in size—but he still played fullback on Farmington's football team. He was also a star basketball player despite his small stature. Dick's religion was sports in all forms.

But it was baseball that took—and under Coach Leo Pinsky, a local state level legend, McAuliffe and his team mates claimed three state championships in a row and together won 411 games. "He was an excellent baseball coach," McAuliffe recalled. "A very tough individual. When you didn't show up for practice, when you didn't run hard, when you didn't hustle, he'd take you right out of the ballgame and sit you down."

Only years later did he fully realize the impact Coach Pinsky had on him. "I thought those were good rules he had, and I think that he gave me a lot of direction."

During his junior year of high school McAuliffe caught the attention of Boston Red Sox scout Joe Dugan at a tryout camp hosted at Bristol's Muzzy Field. Only 16 years old, he was impressive, and Dugan told him to come back the next year when he turned 17. Unfortunately for Dick, the

McAuliffe family was a victim of the 1955 flood that damaged many homes in his hometown and in the Farmington River Valley. Dick spent the year helping rebuild his parents' home rather than returning to Farmington High. He did finish school a year later, leading the Indians baseball team to the state tournament as a pitcher and third baseman. It was an exciting time for Farmington.

"I was pitching a game in the state championship! I always had a good arm in high school," Dick recalled. "My first 11 pitches I threw were all balls. We had two guys on, and a 3-and-0 count on the next hitter, so Pinsky took me out. He put me at third, I made a couple of good plays and got a couple of hits. Detroit Tigers scout Lew Cassell was in the stands during that tournament and McAuliffe recalled their conversation after that.

 "You're not a pitcher, by the way, are you?" Dick remembered Cassell asking.

 "I think he already knew that, but he was pulling my leg. Then he gave me an application to fill out…and about two weeks later, he was in the area,; he called my parents on a Sunday afternoon. He asked if I wanted to sign and play professional baseball…and I said, "Yes, I really do!"

McAuliffe signed shortly after the Class of 1957 graduated, guaranteeing a $500 bonus and an opportunity to play professional ball almost immediately. They made it clear that it was all about production. In the 50s and 60s, baseball management was all about buying and selling positions—not players nor men. They were commodities.

Farmington High School won the state championship in '57, McAuliffe's senior year—

and after that, he was off and running. He had a good solid—though awkward—swing, a good eye on the ball, and was fast around the bags. Through his high school years, he tried his hand as a pitcher, without much success—but his powerful right arm would serve him well… just not from the mound. But it came to pass that from whatever position and from any angle, the baseball scouts started to notice him.

When he returned for his senior year, it was the Tigers who took the most notice, offering him a

$500 signing bonus. At the time, for a young man unaccustomed to such offerings, this seemed a like significant sum. At the age of 17, right after he and

Farmington won State, McAuliffe signed on with the Detroit Tigers as an amateur free agent. Not many get into the Majors straight out of high school! Back then, that was especially true. He had no back up plan and no real interest in college. His was a "Burn the Ships" mentality. He would succeed or die…there was no tryin'! Baseball was his destiny.

During the crucial early growing phase of a ballplayer where habits good and bad are established, he spent three seasons honing his skills in the Tigers' farm system. In 1960, McAuliffe hit an impressive 109 home runs and had 430 defensive assists as shortstop while playing for the Knoxville Smokies in the minor "Sally League." This was the call every ball player dreams of—and something Dick had been working toward since he was in Little League came that fall. He made his major league baseball debut on a fine crisp fall day on September 17, 1960, at Tiger

Stadium in Detroit, Michigan. He was proud to join the number of famous players through the years that have donned the Old English 'D' for the Tigers: Ty Cobb, Mickey Cochrane, Willie Horton and Al Kaline just to name a few.

Growing up in Connecticut McAuliffe was naturally a Red Socks fan with the traditional hatred for the pin-stripers from the Bronx. "I always hated the NY Yankees," he said as a 21-year-old backup Shortstop. "I always thought they had a lot of luck and got a lot of lucky calls from the umpires."

The June 22, 1957, New York Times reported the signing of a promising young "infielder-outfielder from Hartford, Conn." He would immediately report to the 'Erie Sailor's of the Class D New York-Penn League. "I flew from Bradley Field in Hartford to Erie," McAuliffe remembered. "I go to the ballpark … and the team had just left to go on the road to Jamestown, which was a couple-hour bus ride, but they would return that evening." The cab driver took McAuliffe downtown to the team general manager's office. The GM told Dick to go across the street and check into the team hotel, and come back for dinner. "I had my only suit and tie on, thinking he's going to take me out to a fancy restaurant, I get there, and he takes me to the corner drugstore and buys me a 69-cent macaroni and cheese dinner! And then we drive over to Jamestown. … We watched the ballgame and the first thing that came to my mind after I watched … was yes, I can handle this." The 18-year-old played 60 games, mostly at shortstop, had 36 hits, 9 doubles, 16

RBIs, and a .206 batting average. The speed of the pitches was an adjustment for the young infielder. "Don't they throw curves in Unionville, sonny?" he was asked. Charles Kress was the Erie manager, and the Sailors won the league championship, beating the Batavia Indians three games to one!

As for school…McAuliffe could not have been less interested in going to college. He wanted to play—and it was now or never! The MLB would not wait. Looking back he commented on his aggressive style of play, "I always played hard and was very determined, something I learned from my high school coach Leo Pinsky who was very tough and a hustle, hustle coach. I became a scrappy little player—and a damned good one. What carried me through my long career was having determination and desire," he said.

Dick McAuliffe became something of a force to be reckoned with in the minors. During his 1960 season with the Knoxville Smokies, he led the league in runs, triples, and assists. (The Smokies are in the Double-A Southern League but they were a Sally League team in the South Atlantic Double-A League.)

His first few years in the minors also saw McAuliffe get busy off the field. He married a beautiful local girl Joanne Cromack on March 3, 1962, in Hartford, Connecticut. He was 22 she was 20. Shortly thereafter, their daughter Mary

Elizabeth was born in 1963, and soon after that, his son Michael John blessed the family. Dick and Joanne were married for 54 happy years. But let's not get ahead of ourselves in the story…The real question that lay ahead was: Could Dick compete at a professional level and not go crazy in the process? To McAuliffe the game was simple…hit, run, throw, catch…but to the other rookie players, not so much.

CHAPTER 2

Mr. Baseball

"Baseball is a lot like life. It's a day-to-day existence, full of ups and downs. You make the most of your opportunities in baseball as in life."
Tiger Sportscaster Ernie Harwell

"Every time I go out there I tell myself that maybe I'm going to do something today that nobody's ever done before. So I've got to play it to the hilt"
Detroit Tiger Dick McAuliffe

Becoming a truly professional baseball player is a long and challenging process. Playing from the heart and not the pocketbook required a sacrifice of self and McAuliffe started on the road to the majors early in life. Signed by Detroit in 1960, he made his Major League debut with the Tigers as a late Fall call up and played in eight games that year. In 1962, he secured the starting Shortstop position and remained there until moving over to second base at the start of the 1967 season. He then achieved All-Star status three consecutive years (between 1965 and 1967) and was a vital contributor to Detroit's capturing of the world championship in 1968. He participated in a highly productive lineup including Al Kaline, Norm Cash, and Willie Horton. McAuliffe found there were lots of challenges to being a pro ball player: The

The Baseball Players Prayer

Lord, please clear my head of all distractions
and my heart pf burdens I may bear…
so I may perform at my very best,
Knowing you will always be there.

Please left me up before the moment,
so through your eyes I may see, and
have a clearer undetstanding of thy will
as the game unfolds before me.

With great courage I will meet this challenge
as you would have me do. But keep me
humble and remind me that my strenghts
come from knowing you, oh Lord.

Then when all eyes are upon me.
at the end of this game,
I will turn their eyes to you God,
and to the flory of your name…
Amen.

Author Unknown

travel was laborious—not glamorous—but the balls and bags were bright white, and the ball parks were cathedrals…but the PR demands were many and mostly he just missed his family.

"My first year in pro ball, the velocity that the pitchers threw compared to high school was a lot more," lefty batter McAuliffe said. "I was hitting everything to left field. I wasn't getting on the pitches." But Tiger hitting instructor Wayne Blackburn had a fix. "They were floodin' me to the left, and it was difficult, there weren't any holes out there to get hits. So they got me to open up, get my hips out of the way, and pretty much develop the stance that I had, and I was pretty successful with it. I stayed with it that whole spring training and after six or seven weeks of spring training I got really familiar with it, and I was hitting the ball to right field, left field, and up the middle…By the time I left spring training I was very comfortable."

Many compared the new McAuliffe "foot-in-the-bucket" stance to that of Mel Ott, the former New York Giants star. Bill James, who ranked McAuliffe 22nd of all-time among second basemen in his Historical Baseball Abstract, described it this way: "He tucked his right wrist under his chin and held his bat over his head, so it looked as if he were dodging the sword of Damocles in mid-descent. He pointed his left knee at the catcher and his right knee at the pitcher and spread the two as far apart as humanly possible, his

right foot balanced on the toes, so that to have lowered his heel two inches would have pulled his knee inward by a foot. He whipped the bat in a sort of violent pinwheel which produced line drives, strikeouts, fly balls, few ground balls, and not a lot of pop outs." It was odd but it worked.

The work continued and it was back to Class D and Valdosta in the Georgia-Florida League in 1958. The 5-foot-11 shortstop made the all-star team, hitting .286 with 17 doubles, 5 triples, 8 home runs, and 62 RBIs. "I just started progressing," McAuliffe said. "Started hitting for average and hitting with power. I began making less mental and physical mistakes." His fielding still left much to be desired; he tallied 45 errors in 93 games. Under manager Stubby Overmire, Valdosta won the league title over Albany in the playoffs. McAuliffe wasn't around for the postseason however, having been sent up to the Augusta Tigers in the Class A South Atlantic League for the end of the 1958 season. He played 41 games with Augusta, hitting .241 with 13 RBIs—he was 19. The Tigers finished the season in first place but lost in the first round of the Sally League playoffs to the eventual champion, The Macon Dodgers from Georgia.

The 1959 season began for McAuliffe with the Durham Bulls of the Class B Carolina League. He was again an all-star shortstop, despite 35 errors in 94 games with Carl Yastrzemski, the all-star second baseman and league MVP from the pennant-winning Raleigh Capitals who would become McAuliffe's teammate 15 years later. McAuliffe hit .267 for the Bulls, driving in a healthy 43 runs. He finished the season back in the Sally League with the Knoxville Smokies, managed by former Red Sox great Johnny Pesky. "I liked Johnny, his brand of baseball," McAuliffe said. "He was a tough man to play for.

25

You know, a real hard-ass." He played only 11 games for Pesky that year, getting only four hits in 26 at-bats.

In 1960 it was back to Knoxville—this time under manager Frank Skaff. McAuliffe was again a Minor League All Star. His 109 runs scored led the league. He batted .301, hit 27 doubles, a career-

best 21 triples, 7 homers, and drove in 54 runs. McAuliffe was in his groove and earned a promotion to the big lights in September.

The 1960 Detroit Tigers were on their way to a 71-83 record, good for a sixth-place finish in the American League that year—just 26 games behind the pennant-winning Yankees. McAuliffe remembered his first major-league appearance, against the Chicago White Sox on September 17: "It was in Detroit, in a game that I pinch-hit for the pitcher, and we were way behind. The pitcher walked me on four straight pitches, and there was one out at the time…we were behind by a lot of runs. We had no chance of winning the ballgame. So I get on first base, and there's one out, and all I want to do is not make any mistakes out on the bases. So the next batter got up, and hits a real soft line drive to the shortstop, and I don't know what made me do it – I guess the excitement that I was in the big leagues and all the people there and everything — and I just broke loose for second base…and I got tagged out, so it wasn't a very good impression."

Three days later he got his Major League first start against the Indians in Cleveland. "Jim Perry was pitching at home for Cleveland, in Cleveland, and the first three times up I got a single, a triple, and another single. And then Dick Stigman came in, and he was just throwing balloons up there, and he threw one down the middle of the plate and I popped it up. And that was my first big-league out." (McAuliffe evened the score with Stigman in 1961, hitting his first major-league home run off the Indians pitcher on June 23 at Cleveland Stadium.) McAuliffe's defense was still a work in progress in 1960 – in seven games at shortstop, he made only five errors.

At the end of the season, manager Joe Gordon wanted his young shortstop to come to California. "He wanted to take me to Sacramento, where he lived. He wanted to tutor me while I was out there, and he would get me a job at one of the big factories. They have great semipro baseball out there. He wanted me to hook up with one of the teams and play to get in better shape…while I was out there. And at the end of the season, they fired Joe Gordon, so I never did get to go." Bob Scheffing would be brought in for the 1961 season. "The best manager I played for was…Joe Gordon." McAuliffe said. "He was tough, he was fair, and he treated the player…like a man."

McAuliffe started 1961 in the mountain air of Colorado, playing for manager Charlie Metro and the Triple-A Denver Bears. After 64 games with Denver, the 22-year-old shortstop was hitting .353! He made 24 errors, but his hitting earned him a call to the Motor City. Joining the Tiger team for a game against the Washington Senators on June 22, 1961, shortstop Dick McAuliffe was now a Tiger to stay. In July there was some concern that President Kennedy would expand the military draft for Viet Nam, leaving the 21-year-old McAuliffe vulnerable. But it didn't come to pass. He finished a six-month stint in the Air Force Reserves before spring training in 1962. The 1961 Tigers had an excellent campaign, posting a 101-61 record. But during this time, and the Yankees were the dominant team at 109 and 53. McAuliffe played 55 games at shortstop and 22 at third base.

McAuliffe also added a wife and second base to his repertoire in 1962. That season he played 70 games at second base, 49 at third, and 16 at shortstop. He was nothing if not flexible. He made 30 errors, but

more than made up for them when up at home plate, batting .263 with 20 doubles, 12 home runs, and 63 RBIs. He had his first career four-hit game against the Red Sox at Tiger Stadium on May 11. His first child, Mary Elizabeth, was born in 1963.

In the 1960s, McAuliffe was to baseball as John McEnroe was to Pro Tennis years later: Colorful. Folks had never heard the grunts, groans, and emotions that both displayed while playing. It was part of Dick's 'Jekyll and Hyde' personality. On the diamond, he was a fierce vocal competitor—but off field, he had a quiet, almost stately, persona. To him, saying "Hello how are you" was a lengthy conversation. The 1960s was a turbulent time for Detroit and for the nation; he was wondering if all the work and sacrifice would pay off. He was about to find out!

McAuliffe had a reputation throughout his career for having a truly unusual batting stance, which was lovingly described by sports writer and historian Bill James: "He tucked his right wrist under his chin and held his bat over his head, so it looked as if he were dodging the sword of Damocles in mid-descent. He pointed his left knee at the catcher and his right knee at the pitcher and spread the two as far apart as humanly possible, his right foot balanced on the toes, so that to have lowered his heel two inches would have pulled his knee inward by a foot. He whipped the bat in a sort of violent pinwheel producing a variety of hits; line drives, outs, fly balls, and pop outs," he said.

"Whipped the bat in a sort of violent pinwheel" is such a glorious way to describe a man's swing. In addition to being recognizable for his aggressive attitude was his unorthodox batting stance.

"In the minors, I had a hard time adjusting to the velocity of the pitches and I hit everything to left field so they were flooding me on the left side. My coach Wayne Blackburn had me open up my hips and lean back so I could hit the ball where it was pitched and not over stride. At first it was difficult to balance—but once I got used to sitting back and then pivoting, it was no problem." The results were noticeable and it made a difference at the plate.

In 1960, the Tigers Triple-A affiliate, 'The Denver Bears', had finished first in the American League Association. McAuliffe, who was called up from Denver in June 1961, remembers the humor of veteran pitcher Paul Foytack. Foytack loved playing Gin Rummy so much on plane rides, that he'd refuse to stop—even after the plane landed, McAuliffe said. "He'd have one of our teammates hold the cards as they were all still walking and playing," he said. McAuliffe also said the team was always upbeat. "I think the guys were good for one another," he said. "One guy never downgraded anyone on the team. They always rooted for you, and always cheered."

"In any situation, with the talent we had, we could have beaten anybody in any given series," he said.

"Unfortunately, we didn't have the opportunity. But I feel we could have beaten any team if we had the chance." McAuliffe said that, in retrospect, he doesn't remember the 1961 team for failing to win the pennant; instead, it's the camaraderie and friendship that have stayed with him over the years. And it wasn't just on the diamond either.

"When we were out to dinner all we'd do is talk about baseball," he said. "In the later part of my career, guys never did that anymore. Early on we always talked about it, and that was great. They were all good guys and good players."

Getting into the Majors at age 20 was a rarity in his day. A keystone man with power, he topped 20 homers three times in the heart of baseball's Second Deadball Era (a time from 1964 to 1972 when batting averages were unusually low). Thanks to his pronounced uppercut swing, he tied the MLB record by going the entire '68 season without grounding into a double play. Primarily a lead-off hitter, McAuliffe was unmistakable at the plate with his plucky, intense, wide-open batting stance and high Mel Ott-style leg kick. It was quite a sight. Even fifty years later, the Detroit Tigers of 1961 — men now in their 70s and 80s — have not forgotten the season that slipped away. It might have been an immortal year. After all, the team had won as many regular-season games — 101 — as any Detroit team had up to that point. But instead, the "season that wasn't" has been relegated to the footnotes of history, overshadowed by the boys from the Bronx. The NY Yankees dominated sports headlines that summer with Roger Maris and Mickey Mantle captivating the nation while pursuing Babe Ruth's single-season home run record. New York won 109 games—a figure topped only once in the previous three decades—and captured a tenth pennant in 12 years. Exciting times and the stands were full.

"I always had a unique closed stance," McAuliffe told The Courant newspaper in 2010. "The manager, Stubby Overmire, asked me how I'd hit the previous year. I said, 'Not so good.' I was hitting everything to left field. He said, 'Open your hips up...and you'll be able to hit it anywhere you want.'"

McAuliffe became known for his batting stance, one of the most unusual in the history of the game. It was developed in the minors in Valdosta, Georgia, in 1958. McAuliffe, a left-handed hitter, developed the stance — wide open, hands held high and way back, bat flat — for a simple reason: it worked.

McAuliffe's career established him as a go-to infielder and moved along rapidly. In the 1961 and '62 seasons, he shifted between shortstop and second base before becoming the Tigers starting shortstop from 1963–1966. Statistically McAuliffe never hit higher than .275—but he was still a significant contributor to the Tigers' overall offensive output in the 1960s. In 1964, he hit a career-high of 24 home runs, the most by any Tiger player that season.

In 1965 McAuliffe became an All-Star. He was the American League's starting shortstop in the MLB

All Star game, and he went 2-for-3 with a home
run and two runs batted in. Voted the American
League Starter at short, he led off the bottom of the
first at Metropolitan Stadium in Minneapolis

1968 Tiger Player Nicknames

Each of the '68 Tigers had a nickname-most of which were awarded by pitcher Pat Dobson, who was himself known as "Cobra." ...

Norm Cash was "Beagle"
Dick McAuliffe was "Mad Dog"
Earl Wilson was "Duke"
Mickey Stanley was "Squirrely"
Don Wert was "Coyote"
Jim Price was "Big Guy"
Joe Sparma was "Square Deal"
Wayne Comer was "Bush Hog"
Darryl Patterson was "Chief"
Tom Matchick was "Pizza"
Ray Oyler was "Oil Can"
John Hiller was "Ratso"
Willie Horton was "Boomer"
Denny McLain was "Dolphin"
Bill Freehan was "Big Ten"
Jim Northrup was "Fox"
Mickey Lolich was "Condor"
Gates Brown was, of course, "Gator"
Al Kaline was, simply, "Line"

To this day, those nicknames have stuck!

before popping out to shortstop. Against Jim
Maloney in the fourth, McAuliffe singled and later
scored on a Rocky Colavito hit. In the fifth,
McAuliffe faced Maloney again. "He threw me a
high fastball, and in fact it was a funny thing,
because Bill Freehan, our catcher was out in the
bullpen," McAuliffe remembered. "And Bill was
talking to one of the catchers in the NL, and he
was saying, 'How the hell does a guy like
McAuliffe hit with that type of stance?' And no
sooner was it out of his mouth than I hit the ball
over his head [for a two-run homer]. … And
Freehan just turned and said, 'Just like *that!*'"

McAuliffe's numbers fell off a bit in 1965, due in
part to a broken hand that limited him to only 113
games. Still, he hit .260, slammed 15 home runs,
and drove in 54 RBIs. He began a transition into
the leadoff spot that year, batting first in 48 games.

"I was the type of guy who had a pretty good eye
at the plate and got a fair amount of walks,"
McAuliffe said of his leadoff efforts. "My on-base
percentage was always good, so if I'm on base
quite often it gives a chance for the number two,
three, and four hitters to drive me in." He had a
career .343 on-base percentage. He hit quite a few
leadoff home runs then–19 of them, in fact.

Dick and JoAnne's second child, Michael John,
was born in February 1966, right before Spring
Training at 'Tiger Town' in Lakeland, Florida. That

season, illness and injury affected Dick again. He was limited to 124 games, but was again voted the starting Shortstop in the MLB All-Star Game where he went hitless, and struck out. That year he achieved 23 home runs, drove in 56 runs, and brought his average up to .274, a career best.

In 1966, he finished the season ranked fourth in the league with a .373 on-base percentage and fifth in the league with a .509 slugging percentage. Yet to some he might be considered a "second tier" player—but fans loved him. One thing was sure: when he was on the field, there would be no gifts. If you wanted it, you had to come and take it.

When asked why he used an unorthodox batting stance, he stated, "In the minors I had a hard time adjusting to the velocity and at first it was difficult to balance—but once I got used to hanging back and then pivoting it was no problem." His efforts were noticeable and added to Tiger wins.

For McAuliffe, baseball continued—and after making the American League All Star team in 1965 and 1966 at shortstop, he agreed to move to the Tigers second base position in 1967 to make room for Ray Oyler to take over as shortstop. Even with the move to the new position, McAuliffe was selected for his third consecutive All-Star team in 1967. McAuliffe had found his confidence. When a 100 mile per hour fast ball is being thrown at you, it is confidence that makes you swing at a ball going so fast that sometimes you can't even see it!

The 1967 season was memorable for the tight four-way pennant race between the Tigers, the Boston Red Sox, the Minnesota Twins, and the Chicago White Sox, with all four teams still in contention entering the final week of the season. It was a 4-way tie, and the Tigers needed to win the final

game of the season against the California Angels to force a one-game playoff with the Red Sox for the American League championship. Unfortunately, the Tigers lost that game to finish the season a single game behind the Bo Sox. Along with Al Kaline and Bill Freehan, McAuliffe played an integral role for the Tigers during the 1967 season, finishing among the American League leaders in walks with 105 (3rd), 245 times on base (3rd), along with 7 triples (3rd), 92 runs (5th), 118 strikeouts (5th), 22 home runs (8th), and a .364 on-base percentage (9th). Yet these high stats were not enough for some in the media nor Tiger Management. And while excitement ruled the day in baseball at Michigan and Trumble, the summer of 1967 saw Detroit in flames of racial tension. The riots in Detroit that summer were the bloodiest urban riots in history, costing 43 lives, with 1189 wounded and more than $40 million in damages. It was a sad time for the city despite Tiger successes.

In 1967, McAuliffe replaced the fading Jerry Lumpe at Tiger second base. That season, the All-Star Game Starters were chosen by the players. Rod Carew was tapped to start at second. McAuliffe came into the game in the seventh. He flied to right in the eighth, again in the 11th, and once again in the 14th inning – his final career All-Star at-bat. The American League lost, 2-1 in the 14th inning. For McAuliffe, 1967 was another fine offensive year hitting in the top third of the order. Twenty-two home runs, a career-high 105 walks, and 65 RBIs helped the Tigers to a 91-71 record and set up an epic battle down to the final out of the season.

He set a major-league record the next season when he didn't ground into a double play during the entire season. "I wasn't quick…I was fast," McAuliffe told interviewer Peter Zanardi in the early 1990s, "I could get down to first base; being left-handed, I had a quick start at home plate. But one thing that helped me…was leading off so many times with nobody on base." The lead off position is essential to producing runs; when the first batter gets on base, the rest of the lineup then drives them home.

On the last play of the regular season, McAuliffe, representing the tying run, grounded into a double play, and dashed Detroit's hopes of clinching a tie for the American League pennant. Despite the Detroit riots and the great disappointment of the '67 season, the groundwork for a world championship had been laid.

Chapter 3

Champions: The '68 Tigers

"I love sports! Whenever I can, I always watch the Detroit Tigers on the radio."
President Gerald R. Ford

"90% of this game is half mental!"
Manager/Player Yogi Berra

After the '67 riots, Detroit was a divided and hurting community. Both the Black and White communities were in mourning. My cousins and Uncle, all Detroit firefighters, told harrowing stories about one building burned to the ground with the business next door untouched. The only difference was the phrase "Soul Brother" in white shoe polish on the unbroken large window. They told tales of having a fire hose in one hand and a

43

"Dick McAuliffe was the kind of player you could always count on, and you know he will cover your back!"
Detroit Tiger Gates 'Gator' Brown

semi-machine gun in the other. Although professional baseball started to racially integrate after WW2, the Tigers were one of the last MLB teams to fully integrate. Detroit, being a predominately Black city, had few racial problems —but in Lakeland, Florida, which was home to 'Tiger Town' and spring training, it was a completely different story. Black players and their families had to endure substandard housing with no air conditioning and local attitudes that were… how shall I said it? Locals were less than cordial. The Tiger players and their families were a tight knit group, and some say that it was Dick's wife who helped the Tiger wives establish and maintain a sense of community as well as lead the way to eliminating racial restrictions and improving living conditions for everyone during spring training.

In 1967, racial integration and "Bussing" were at the forefront of the national discussion. While the '67 pennate race slipped out of reach of the Tigers, the city lay smoldering from the riots and from racial division. Some found it interesting that in the middle of a "Black city" lay a 3-block area near Michigan Ave. and Tumble that suburban

Whites felt comfortable and safe enough to regularly visit the stadium 'downtown'.

With the groundwork of '67, Detroit easily won the American League pennant in 1968. McAuliffe led the league that year with 95 runs. He also finished 7th in the AL Most Valuable Player voting. In the World Series, the Tigers came back from a long shot 3-games-to-1 deficit to upset the defending world champion St. Louis Cardinals. It was their first world championship since just after WW2 in 1945. McAuliffe's performance was impressive, as he smacked in a home run and drove in three runs throughout the series.

But as disappointing as '67 was, it was a good precursor to victory. "We knew we should have won. We lost the pennant on the last day of the

season—but we were determined to win it all the next year," McAuliffe said. It was obvious some mistakes were made. "I loved Mayo Smith [the Tiger Manager], he had a great personality and guys liked him; but he wasn't the best manager in the world," he said. "I had the most fun in baseball in 1968 because the guys all clicked both on and off the field. Everybody played as a team and it was wonderful."

In the Tigers' 1968 World Championship season, McAuliffe played a key role. He had a .344 on-base percentage, led the American League with 95 runs scored, and showed power with 50 extra base hits. He also tied a major league record by going the entire 1968 season without grounding into a double play—and he is the only American League player who has done so to this day. McAuliffe also improved defensively in 1968, reducing his error total from 28 in 1967 to nine in 1968, and finished second among American League second basemen in fielding percentage.

He had a reputation for toughness; he was the Tigers' catalyst in their 1968 World Championship campaign, he played all seven games in the World Series, in which the Tigers claimed the championship by defeating the St. Louis Cardinals 4 games to 3. He was the AL's starting shortstop in the 1965 and 1966 All-Star games, and was an All-Star second baseman in 1967. This was quite a record—and yet it was not enough for the sports writers of the day to take notice, as they continued to overlook his accomplishments as did Tiger management. They were lucky he loved the game.

In the 1968 World Championship season, he tied a Major League record by going the entire year without hitting into a double play. His unorthodox wide open batting stance of leaning back in the box with the front foot "in the bucket" and the bat cocked at his head was often imitated by his many young fans on the playground. Rare among middle infielders of his day, McAuliffe also had power—and upon retiring, he finished among Detroit's All-Time Top Ten in five offensive categories. He finished seventh in the balloting for the league's Most Valuable Player award in 1968. His teammate Denny McLain, who won 31 games at the head of a formidable pitching staff that also included Mickey Lolich, who was named MVP that year. If he was disappointed not to be recognized, McAuliffe did not show it. He never did. It was part of his stoic nature at times.

In 1968, "[McAuliffe] was the guy who made us go," said Gates 'Gator' Brown, an outfielder and an extraordinary pinch-hitter for the Tigers, as quoted by Tim Wendel in his 2012 book "Summer of '68". The 1968 Detroit Tigers ran away with the American League pennant, finishing 103-59, 12 games ahead of the runner-up, Cleveland. "We were absolutely phenomenal for that particular year," McAuliffe remembered. "I mean, when you think a guy like Denny McLain won 31 ballgames

…but it was more than that. We averaged five plus runs for Denny throughout that year. Mickey Lolich was also a great pitcher for our team, won 17 ballgames, but the key factor I think is that everybody contributed at the right time and way."

There were other elements to that season, however. Al Kaline was in the outfield, and was "the best right fielder you'd ever want to see," according to McAuliffe. "Never made a mistake in the outfield, never dropped a ball, always threw to the right base. Quick release, not only a strong arm, but very accurate." Norm Cash, "the comic of our ball club," slugged 25 home runs. Meanwhile, Willie Horton led the team with 36, and outfielder Jim Northrup drove in 90 runs. Bill Freehan was "a good catcher, excellent with knowing how to pitch teams…he was a good, solid man behind the plate. Freehan knew how to call a ballgame, knew the pitchers that he had."

Of manager Mayo Smith, McAuliffe said, "I don't call him a great manager, but… I think the biggest plus that he asserted to the club was that…he would have everybody moving on the bases. No matter who was on base. If a guy was on first and second and the count was 3-and-1 or 3-and-2, you'd be running. We were so successful with it that it was unbelievable. We'd stay out of double plays, we'd put the bat on the ball and we got base hits… it created the spark!"

That season McAuliffe reduced his errors and he was shocked that he didn't win the MLB 'Gold Glove' that year—while California Angle Bobby Knoop, who made 15 errors, did. Many, including myself, thought McAuliffe had been robbed. He hit 95 home runs, 24 doubles, 10 triples, and 16 home runs, drove in 56 runs, and hit .249. He played in his first World Series against St. Louis. His offensive stats weren't the most impressive, but he didn't make any errors in the Tigers' winning the seven-game World Series.

Years later, McAuliffe always underplayed his role and like he wasn't a key element to the team's overall success. "Everybody on the team contributed and I would have to say that (next to my kids being born) the 1968 season with the Tigers was the highlight of my life!"

Chapter 4

Mad Dog, the Hustler

"Every strike brings me closer to a home run."
Babe Ruth

"There's no crying in baseball!"
A League of Their Own

Dick McAuliffe's nickname was simultaneously both accurate and a non-sequitur; on the field, he was a fierce competitor—while off the field, he was a pure gentleman with small town sensibilities. Dick McAuliffe was living proof that someone with a little talent could go far and compete with the best of them by using all the gifts God has given them. That is not to say his talents were not substantial…they were. But he had a strong old fashioned work ethic.

When asked about his grandpa's attitude and disposition, JP Boyle, Dick McAuliffe's grandson, is upfront. "Like most Italian/Irish men he could have a bit of a temper at times…and he had a low tolerance for B.S. He had no time for putting on airs or trying to impress people, and [had] little tolerance for those who did. He never wanted folks to think he was special just because he was a pro ball player," JP explained. "Like for example, when trying to get a table at a fancy restaurant or tickets to a show…he would never bring up who he was, or that he was famous. He just wasn't like that," he said. McAuliffe was nothing if not self-effacing and humble.

Primarily a lead-off hitter, McAuliffe was unmistakable at the plate with his plucky and unusual batting stance. A left-handed hitter, McAuliffe held his hands very high with an open stance that faced the pitcher. As the pitcher delivered to home plate, he moved his forward (right) foot to a more conventional position before swinging. The wide-open batting stance and being a middle infielder with power saw him reach twenty homers three times in his career.

A player's player and team rally igniter during their Championship year and throughout his time with the team, he led the team and League and showed his fortitude again the following season, hitting a pinch homer in his last at-bat before being forced onto the disabled list with a knee injury. Despite lacking truly exceptional natural ability, he was still a three-time AL All-Star—and despite having no accolades to his name, he was an essential component to the winning team.

The 1960s was a time of change; one story talks about a young female newspaper reporter named Mary Weston. She was covering the Tigers during the 1968 season. She was one of the first female reporters to do so and had to endure a number of suggestive and derogatory comments from Tiger players. When the PR flap happened and it appeared it was going to be a black eye for the team, Tiger management sent McAuliffe and Pat Dobson to try and smooth things over…and they did so. It was known that Dick could talk to anyone about most anything. This made him a good diplomat. Weston never mentioned how she had been treated and McAuliffe and Dobson, along with Tiger Management, let it be known

that it was not to happen again. And it didn't.

As a mainstay in the Tiger's middle infield throughout the 1960s, the three-time All-Star was a hard-nosed player few would mess with. On August 22, 1968, McAuliffe was involved in a career defining brawl with Chicago White Sox pitcher Tommy John. This is the incident that earned him the nickname "Mad Dog" after charging the mound.

Years later McAuliffe recalled the well-documented run-in with White Sox pitcher Tommy John like it was yesterday. "In the first inning, I got a hit and scored from second on Al Kaline's hit. I was a pest on the bases, and I scored a lot of runs. Tommy John was a sinker slider, [a] low ball

pitcher—but my next time up, he threw two right at my head. On 3 and 2, I was looking for a good pitch to hit but he threw a ball over my head to the backstop giving me a walk. I am sure the orders not to give me anything to hit came from his manager, Eddie Stanky. I wasn't going to charge

the mound, so I dusted myself off and glanced at him when I was trotting down to first. When he took two steps in to get a new ball, he said, 'What the fuck are *you* looking at?' Then all I saw were stars…and I ran out to the mound. As I charged, he lowered himself into me and broke his collarbone." John was out for the season, and Dick was suspended for five games, matches that would make a real difference in the Tiger march towards the championship.

Interviewed 30 years later, McAuliffe was still convinced John was throwing at his head. "The first pitch at me was right at my head, and I mean right at my head. The catcher never laid any leather on it, and it hit the backstop. The next pitch, he spun me down, threw it behind me," he said. White Sox' general manager Ed Short took a different view, pointing out the pitch before the fight came on a 3-2 count, resulting in a runner reaching base. The next pitch however, John threw hard—spinning McAuliffe around with one pitch and hitting the backstop with another. "Boy, if that thing hit me it would really put me away," he told home plate umpire Al Salerno. With the count at 3-2, McAuliffe dug in, thinking there was no way John was going to throw at him again. But the next pitch sailed over McAuliffe's head and hit the backdrop with a huge thud.

"And now I'm mad," McAuliffe recalled, "but not mad enough to go out and charge him." That quickly changed. "I don't know how many times I thought about it that night. I was always able to keep it under control on the field, just barely sometimes…" McAuliffe explained. "I was never

the guy in the middle of a brawl but there was no doubt in my mind that John was throwing right at me, and he was doing so under orders…something just snapped," he said.

Like a charging bull exploding out of the chute, McAuliffe ran at John, who awkwardly tried to tackle him. Both hit the ground as the benches emptied out onto the field. With players, coaches, and umps suddenly converging on the field, John emerged from the fight doubled over, clutching his left shoulder. He was out for the rest of the season, ending a solid campaign of a 10-5 record with a 1.98 ERA. After order was restored, Salerno tossed McAuliffe out of the game. He was replaced by Tiger Ray Oyler. Dennis Ribant came in to pitch for the Sox and wound up taking the loss in a 4-2 Tigers victory. The following day, American League president Joe Cronin ordered an immediate five-game suspension and a $250 fine for

McAuliffe. After Chicago complained that it was too small a fine, it was increased to $500.

In the flurry of charges and countercharges that followed, John insisted the last pitch had simply slipped out of his hand, an explanation nobody in Detroit was buying. McAuliffe's importance was underscored by the team's dismal performance without him in the lineup. The Tigers lost all but one of the five games McAuliffe was forced to sit out, and each game was lost by only a single run. The team used it as a motivator—and the Tigers went on to win the American League pennant and the 1968 World Series.

Of course, pitcher Tommy John remembers the incident very differently. "I was 10 and 5 with a 1.98 ERA and pitching against the Tigers in August. A 3-and-2 pitch slipped out of my hand and sailed over Dick McAuliffe's head. I didn't throw at him, but McAuliffe was yelling at me as he went to first, and he charged the mound," John said. "McAuliffe drove his knee into my left shoulder and separated it."

"John hit us four times in Chicago in June," said Detroit manager Mayo Smith. "They hit eight of our guys in the series there and we didn't hit any of theirs." Despite the Chicago's manager's calls to walk McAuliffe, Tigers' general manager Jim Campbell said, "Cronin simply used bad judgment." It was a heat of the moment call.

There was only one HBP (Hit By Pitch) in that entire four-game series and it was when the Tigers' Pat Dobson hit Pete Ward. The "John game" was the last game of the series. John did hit four Tigers in a game on June 15, though he pitched against them again on June 30 and pitched a five-hit shutout with no HBPs…which only served to make the incident on Aug. 22 even more egregious. But the Tiger train was not to be derailed…they were hot and headed to the American League playoffs. Heady times.

The players on the 1968 Detroit Tigers team became local heroes…some say they even saved the city from itself in a time of tumult and unrest. Certainly after the maelstrom of 1967 and the race riots, Detroit and its sports fans were broken—so the good news story of the Tigers was a way for fans, be they Black or White, suburbanite or urbanite, to rally around the good 'ol hometown team. And it was a remarkable turnaround from the racial problems the year before.

On that hot August night, good friend and fellow Tiger, first baseman "Stormin Norm" Cash, the hard-drinking Texan, was the one that bestowed the nick name upon McAuliffe. "Damn, Dick—you were a Mad Dog out there tonight!" It stuck.

Baseball at the Corner!
1896 - 1999

Navin Field

Briggs Stadium

Tiger Stadium

Chapter 5

Tiger Stadium

Built: 1911
Capacity: 53,000
Longest Center Field in MLB at 440ft
Surface: Michigan Bluegrass
Hosted three MLB All Star Games
Detroit Lions Home 1938-1974

I t was the Cathedral of the Diamond, a
neighborhood hub, and our community
touchstone. A century of baseball, memories,
and fun, professional baseball was first played at
the corner of Michigan and Trumbull on April 28,
1896 in a neighborhood called Corktown. Over the
years, fans flocked to see their heroes—and not
just from Detroit proper, from Grand River to
Woodward—but from 50-75 miles out into the
suburbs of Farmington Hills, Redford, Pontiac,
Monroe, and Mount Clemens…Tiger Stadium and
the other monikers before it, Navin

Field and Briggs
Stadium, was the
place where
Detroiters'
collective memories
reside. Still does.
Everyone has a
story told through
the years of the
happy times at the
ballpark in 1968 and
the entire season of
1984—and the sad
times too, like the
1961 and 1967
seasons when they
came sooooo close.

Built in 1911 out of
Pennsylvania steel

brought by huge ships on the Great Lakes and
cement from the quarries of Indiana, "The Corner"
saw baseball through WW1, the great Depression,
WWII, and the 1950s. In 1961, financier John
Fetzer purchased the ball club and changed the
park's name to Tiger Stadium. But baseball was
not the only sport played at "The Corner." The
National Football League's Detroit Lions played

there from 1938 to 1974 and there were others like
a soccer league; in fact, there were lots of special
events—like when the stadium's field played host
to Anheuser-Busch's Bud Bowl in 2006 or the
numerous concerts there. I saw the Beach Boys

there in 1992 and the Eagles' "Hell Freezes Over" Tour in '94. In the end, the stadium had hosted 6,873 regular season games, 35 postseason contests, and three All-Star Games.

The stadium was very well built and had some unique features like seats that were some of the closest in the majors, putting attendees almost on the field, as well as second deck seats providing an aerial view, and the overhang which provided crucial shade in July and August. The "Bleachers" had their own entrance, concession stands,

restrooms, and protocol. It had a wild, free-sprit feel of being a non-stop party in the sun.

Tiger fans sitting in the bleachers for $4 listening to a radio had better seats than the folks behind

home plate paying ten
times as much. The park
also featured one of the
longest Center Fields in
Baseball at 440ft and
over the years saw
11,111 home runs.

Tiger Stadium was
declared a State of
Michigan Historic Site
in 1975. By the early
1990s, the owner of the
Tigers wanted a new
luxurious ballpark for
the team. After much
wrangling and despite
public opposition, the
last game at the corner
of Michigan Avenue and

Trumble was played in September of 1999 before a
sold out crowd. Some cried. Some stole small
pieces of the lawn to plant at home. The
demolition of Tiger Stadium was completed in
2009—but a Police Athletic League ball field is
now on the site; so in a way, the tradition of
baseball at the corner of Michigan Avenue and
Trumble continues on.

I will never forget as long as I live being 10 years
old and walking out of those dark tunnels, up the
ramp and seeing that green grass diamond, those

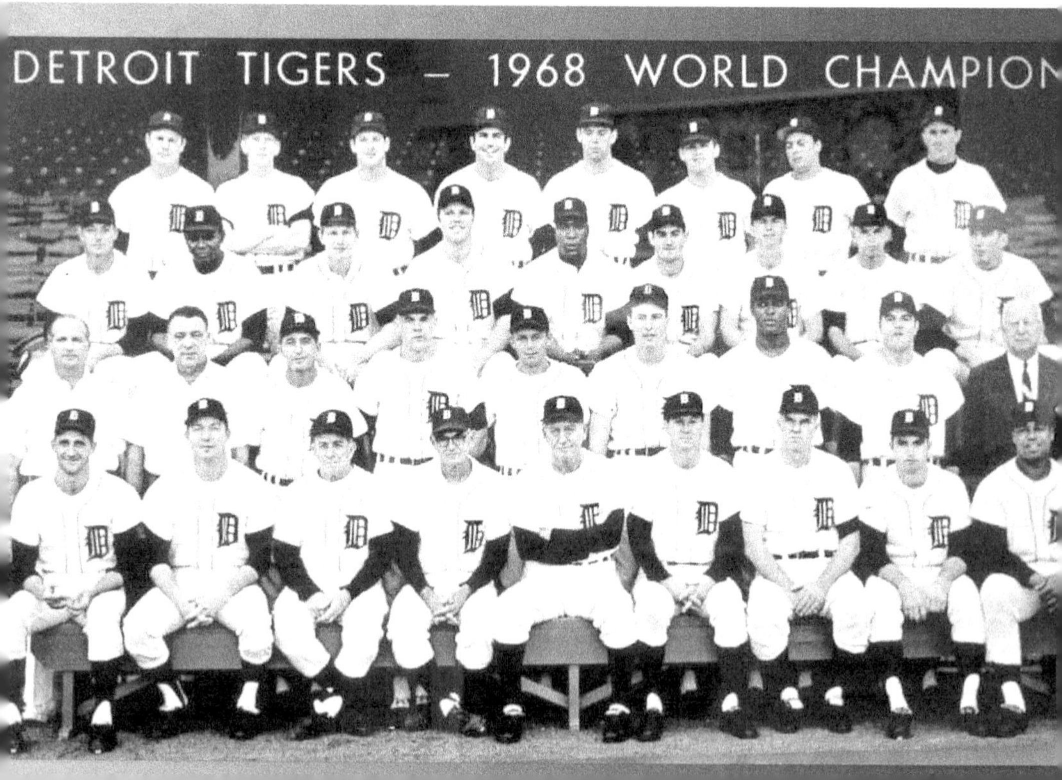

bleached white bases and smelling the peanuts, hot dogs, and beer for the very first time. It was heaven—and when the Tigers hit my first home run and folks jumped up and down with thunderous results and the stadium rumbling…I think I wet my pants! The New Comerica Tiger

stadium opened in 2000 in downtown Detroit near Greek Town. It is indeed gorgeous but…all the luxury boxes, food courts, and spiffiness in the world will never replace my memories of roasting hot dogs, peanuts, and the history in the making with Tiger baseball at 'The Corner'.

Chapter 6

Bottom of the 9th

"Men do not quit playing because they grow old;
they grow old because they quit playing."
Oliver Wendell Holmes

"Later in life I again realized I had a real
champion of a Dad as he became a Dad
to my kids as well."
Daughter Mary McAuliffe-Boyle

"I always played hard and was very determined, something I learned from my high school coach. What carried me through my long career was having determination and desire," he explained. But even strong desire is not enough; to perform a profession athlete needs a strong body unchallenged by injury. After all the parades, parties, and the highs of 1968 and being a world series championship team were done, it was time to get back to work.

The problem was apparent at Spring Training in Lakeland Florida the following year. McAuliffe's knee injury and subsequent surgery derailed

almost his entire season in 1969, limiting the 29-year-old to playing only 74 games. But even while injured, he was still able to produce 11 homers and 33 RBIs! Knee problem and all, he matched 1968s total with only nine field errors.

He would play four more years with Detroit, never again reaching the heights of the 1960s. By 1973, he was a "platoon player," sharing time at second base with Tiger Tony Taylor. It was a bit depressing for the veteran infielder--but as long as he was playing, Dick was happy. But Father Time continued to send hints that the career of the now seasoned veteran was closer to the end than the beginning. On July 15, 1973, the Tigers hosted the California Angels and new red-hot pitcher Nolan Ryan. "Ryan was tough," McAuliffe said. "Back then you couldn't dig in against him, not like today. But that day it was the best stuff I've ever seen from a pitcher in my whole career." As if to prove the point in his three at-bats, the young pitcher fanned Dick three times. And the rest of the Tigers tribe didn't fare any better as Ryan threw his second no-hitter of the 1973 season.

McAuliffe made one more post season appearance, back at shortstop for four games and at second for one game in the 1972 American League Championship series against the Oakland A's. He hit only .200 for the series—but he hit a big home run off Catfish Hunter in Detroit's game four win. The A's won the series in five games. It was his only other postseason appearance… at least with the Tigers. But baseball was not done yet.

McAuliffe continued as the Tigers' starting second baseman through the '73 season. But late in the season he was unceremoniously traded from the Tigers to the Boston Red Sox on October 23, 1973. The next season McAuliffe hit .210 in 100 games for the Red Sox in 1974. The next year he briefly played with the 1975 BoSox team, capturing the

American League Pennant. As both he and management had decided his playing days were over, he began the 1975 season as the manager of Boston's Double-A farm team, the Bristol Red Sox, located in McAuliffe's native state of Connecticut. He guided Bristol into first place in the Eastern League but was recalled to Boston in August to briefly resume his playing career as a utility infielder. However, McAuliffe was released after playing only seven more games for the Sox.

His professional Baseball career ended on September 1, 1975, in a Yankees-Red Sox game. McAuliffe dropped an easy popup for an error. Later in the inning, McAuliffe's throw pulled Carl Yastrzemski off the bag. Though it was scored a single, the Boston fans booed McAuliffe. He was left off Boston's post-season roster, and without fanfare or notice his major league career was over.

He had a decent season for both the Tigers and the Red Socks in 1973, playing in 106 games, hitting .274, and slamming 12 homers. But at age 34, he knew the end was near. "I wanted to move back East, so I told them I wasn't coming back," McAuliffe said. "I wasn't pressuring [the Tigers] into trading me to Boston, but I knew my career was near the end, and I wanted to maybe make a connection and get into business of some sort back there in Connecticut…and Detroit obliged me. Towards the end of the season, I had it out with Tiger GM Jim Campbell and told him 'you guys never treated me fair financially.' I was half way down the payroll and there were guys making more money who hadn't been there as long as I had. I knew I didn't have too much left, but I wanted to get a little bit of a reward. He said, 'No, that's not our policy.' I told Campbell I wouldn't be back next year. I wanted to finish my career in Detroit, and would have—if Campbell had come through. He later called me and asked if I wanted to go to Boston which was closer to my home, and

I said that was fine. I just wish I had finished my career with the Tigers." So does every Tiger fan.

On October 23, 1973, the Red Sox announced that they had acquired the veteran infielder for young outfielder Ben Oglivie. Manager Darrell Johnson expected McAuliffe to challenge Doug Griffin for the second-base job at best, and at worst, back up Rico Petrocelli at third. McAuliffe would wear number 3 for Boston, a number worn by another Connecticut-born Red Sox player, Walt Dropo. McAuliffe was excited about playing at Fenway Park. "It's a great stadium to play in because like Tiger Stadium the fans are so close to you. Just has that special aroma in the air." As for the Boston fans? "They are very, very critical, very tough. But they know the game. They really do."

Things didn't work out exactly as BoSox Manager Johnson had planned. McAuliffe played a utility role in 1974, playing 53 games at second base, 40 at third, three at Shortstop, and three as the designated hitter. He batted only 272 times, and hit .210 with five home runs. It was clear that at age 34, the end had come. He retired at the end of the season, and accepted a Red Sox offer to manage in their minor-league system.

So perhaps a career of team management was in the future. Muzzy Field in Bristol, Connecticut, was only a 20-minute commute from McAuliffe's home and was the source of the Bristol Red Sox of the Double-A Eastern League. Under manager Dick McAuliffe in 1975, Bristol went 81-57. They swept the Reading Pennsylvania Phillies to capture the Eastern Minor League championship.

McAuliffe wasn't around to taste the champagne, however. In August, Red Sox third baseman Rico Petrocelli was suffering from headaches, inner-ear trouble, and vertigo—possibly the result of a 1974 beaning at the plate. The 32-year-old Petrocelli left the Sox in Chicago on August 17, at the time hitting .241 with four home runs and 44 RBIs. Some wondered if his career, much less the 1975 season, was over. As he was placed on the disabled list, Bob Heise was installed as the third baseman, and McAuliffe was pulled from his managerial job in Bristol as back up. "I'm in good shape," he told Peter Gammons of The Sporting News. "I'm seven pounds lighter than I was. I've been throwing in batting practice every day so my arm's strong, my legs are in good condition, and I've been hitting well off and on."

When Petrocelli went down, the Sox inquired about the readiness of Butch Hobson. "Butch had a pretty good bat for me all year long," McAuliffe said as his coach. "But in the field he'd make an awful lot of mistakes. Especially throwing mistakes. And I didn't think he was ready right then. So they asked me, 'Would you be interested in coming up?' There was about six weeks left in the season, and the Red Sox had a big lead in the AL East. "I really didn't think about it, and I said, 'Well, yeah, I would be.' Six weeks or so, you know, it's not long." But the veteran hadn't been completely honest with the parent club or the press. "The only bad thing about it was I wasn't in great shape," McAuliffe said some 15 years later. "I hadn't picked up a bat all year. I threw batting practice out the window — the only thing that was in good shape was my arm."

McAuliffe played in seven games, all at third base, making his first appearance as a defensive replacement on August 23. He batted 15 times, with only two singles (.133). His career ended on a sour note on September 1. The Red Sox were hosting the Yankees, and the 36-year-old McAuliffe started the game at third, batting eighth. With one out in the second, Yankees designated hitter Walt Williams hit a popup between third and home. McAuliffe dropped the ball for an error. With one run in, shortstop Fred Stanley tapped a ball to third, and McAuliffe's throw pulled first baseman Carl Yastrzemski off the bag. It was scored a single, and another run came in. McAuliffe drove in a run, but the Red Sox lost the game, 4-2, and Dick McAuliffe's Major League career was suddenly over. "I never, ever remember being booed in the big leagues," he said, "but in that one game everything stood out. And I really felt bad after that and that was the only time after making an error that I felt really bad about losing a ballgame. And I said, 'Well, I guess I am over the hill.'" The Red Sox obviously agreed—and McAuliffe was left off the postseason roster for the classic 1975 World Series.

The Red Sox wanted McAuliffe to manage in their system in 1976, but he had had enough. It was not just about the money. "You know, the salary wasn't very big (his 1968 salary was approximately $35,000 with a $10,000 World Series bonus). And although I enjoyed doing what I did, it was tough being on the road again after years of playing and leaving your family…and I said that's enough."

He began 1975 as the Manager of Boston's Double-A farm team, the Bristol Red Sox, located in McAuliffe's native state of Connecticut. He guided Bristol into first place in the minor Eastern League. But he could not keep away from the

game, and later McAuliffe played professional softball for the "New England Pilgrims" of the American Professional Slo-Pitch League (APSPL) in their 1979 season.

In the final game of his career, on September 1, 1975, in a game between the Red Sox and the Yankees, an ugly throw to Carl Yastrzemski resulted in the Boston home crowd loudly booing McAuliffe, who had also dropped an easy pop-out earlier in the game. He would ultimately never play professional ball again, and sadly his last

memory of the sport he loved would be a crowd of boos from the fans of his own team. It was an inauspicious end to a once glorious career. He later said, "That one game everything stood out, and the fans in Boston were tough. And I really felt bad after that and that was the only time after making an error that I felt really bad about losing a ballgame. And I said to myself, 'Well, I guess I really *am* over the hill.'"

Chapter 7

PAR, Wash & Camp

*"20 years from now you'll be more disappointed
by the things you didn't do
than by the things you did."*
Mark Twain

*"I knew when my career was over. In 1965, my
baseball card came out with no picture!"*
Bob Uecker

At age 45, McAuliffe retired from professional baseball—but he was busier in "retirement" than he ever was in baseball. In reality, the game was not done with him yet. Shortly after retiring, he created McAuliffe Baseball School, teaching youngsters the finer points of the game. Then he bought a business that repaired and installed coin-operated washers and driers. "I did quite well with it," said McAuliffe. "I was in the laundry business over 10 years…and then got tired of doing it." He sold the business at a profit after 10 years. Later he would be involved with Baseball Fantasy camps where adults could live out their dreams of being professional ballplayers.

"Dad was always into something…At one point or another after he left the Majors he owned a diner, a bakery, baseball camps for the young and Baseball

Fantasy Camps for adults, a coffee services company, a few laundry mats, and a laundry coin machine service business. Even after baseball, he was a busy guy!" explained his daughter Mary. "But in retirement, Dad really loved and enjoyed golf and became quite good at it. Both he and my Mom also loved being snowbirds in the winter down in Florida near Naples." It was a good life.

He and Mrs. McAuliffe made many friends in the sunshine state and Dick belonged to several golf clubs in Florida and played in many charitable golf

events there. A PAR golfer, the natural left handed swinger played golf right handed with a cross handed grip. Perhaps his unusual baseball stance can help to explain why his golf swing was also so unorthodox. "I caddied as a kid, and on Mondays we could play on the course. Being left-handed, I had never seen a left-handed golfer or even a left-handed club. I had to play with right-handed clubs

—but I still gripped it left-handed…just brought it over to the right side," he said. "I just got used to it and was pretty good. I can still drive about 280 yards and I became a scratch golfer. (One whose handicap is zero and hits par.)"

Towards the end of his life one of his favorite memories was seeing his fellow players from '68 while participating in the ceremonies at the closing of Tiger Stadium in 1999. "Being there again was wonderful but you hated to see such a great stadium be retired," he said. "But you know, life has to go on. To me there was nothing like Tiger Stadium, and those Detroit fans. They were devoted fans and good people." Dick always made time for the fans.

Would he have changed anything in his career? "I think the only mistake I made was I should have stayed in Detroit, where I felt more comfortable, and finished up there," McAuliffe said. "They would have given me a job in the minor leagues either as a hitting instructor – or in the big leagues – or perhaps managing in the minor leagues, which would have been fine by me as long as they gave me a decent salary!" he chuckled.

His passion for the Diamond was obvious throughout his life—but folks that knew him would say that his greatest joy was always his family. As a loving father and grandfather, "Papa" was always their biggest supporter and was always there for his daughter, son, and the grandkids.

JP Boyle, Dick's grandson, works in Security and Public Safety. He has one son, age 6, who he's teaching the intricacies of T-Ball baseball with a good dose of Soccer thrown in for good measure. He has fond memories of his grandpa. "Naturally, growing up, it was very cool having a grandpa that was a former Major League Baseball player. I talked about it to my friends all the time…well, as much as they'd let me!" he said with a laugh. "He was always willing to help folks enjoy the game and he was always there for me. For example, he was the Assistant Coach for my and my brothers Little League softball teams. How many other kids could say that a World Series winning baseball player was their coach? None!," said JP. "Farmington is a small, tight knit community and my Grandpa was and is still one of the town's heroes. I was not lucky enough to inherit his baseball skills. I played little league, but soccer was really my passion," he explained.

When you ask her what the best thing about her Dad was, his daughter Mary has to think on it to pick only one thing. "He was just such a humble and down-to-earth guy who love to goof around, have fun and make others laugh, which he often did. But that is not to say that he didn't have a temper or couldn't be stubborn. He could…when he set his mind on something he really focused on it," she explained. "In hindsight? I think he was too hard on himself and felt guilty about not spending enough time with us." Added grandson JP Boyle, "If there was one thing about my grandfather I'd want folks to know it would be that he loved three things in his life: his family, golf and baseball."

His daughter's two sons and he had a special relationship. "My grandpa was a selfless man who always put his family first. He was easy to talk to and whenever I had a problem or needed some advice, I could always count on him to be there for me," shared JP. "I have fond memories of him teaching me how to drive a car and how to catch fish. He was really a father figure to me," JP recalled. "He always had a smile for everyone and had a great sense of humor with the ability to make others laugh. He was just such fun to be around."

Growing up with a professional baseball player as a dad was also special for his daughter, Mary McAuliffe-Boyle. "Naturally, we saw lots of games and ate lots of popcorn. And of course, being able to go to Florida in spring every year was cool! Also, the Tiger players' wives and families was a real community," she said. "It was great to be behind the scenes and while I knew my dad was famous, to me he was just 'my Dad.'" She was 11 years old in 1974 when her father retired from baseball, but she recalls it well.

McAuliffe passed his passion for baseball on to the young and old alike. He enjoyed running The McAuliffe Baseball School teaching kids how to play. "If you've got the desire, you don't need to have superstar skills. The game was very important to me," McAuliffe said. "I took it to heart. I played as hard as I could. I always thought I gave 100 percent and was proud of my skills. I think I should have done better. That's just my personal feeling. But overall, I've been successful."

Afflicted with Alzheimer's' Dick McAuliffe, husband, father, grandfather and pro baseball player, died in Connecticut on May 13, 2016, at the age of 76. He had been struggling with the disease through his later years, a heartbreaking similarity he shared with fellow 1968 Tiger Bill Freehan. At the end, Alzheimer's erased his most cherished memories. "When my Dad got Alzheimer's it was bad. The disease robs you of your memories—and inside of five years, he was gone. It was very sad for everyone," explained his daughter Mary. "When he passed hundreds of players and fans paid their respects from around the world." As well they should have.

Chapter 8

Which Way to Cooperstown?

*"I see great things in baseball. It's our game, the
American game. It will repair our losses
and be a blessing to us all."*
Walt Whitman Quote in Movie 'Bull Durham'

*"Baseball is a lot like life. It's a day-to-day
existence, full of ups and downs. You make the
most of your opportunities in baseball as in life."*
Tiger Sportscaster, Ernie Harwell

If a man can be summed up in stats, his were
significant. Not stellar, necessarily—but of note. In
1,763 career regular season games, he compiled
1,530 hits, with lifetime .247 batting average. But
his was a contribution unquantifiable in statistical
numbers. His was the spark that made the Tiger
engine go. His was the inspiration that motivated
his fellow players to achieve their very best. Dick
McAuliffe had that undefinable trait that is seldom
acknowledged nor rewarded but without it a team
is just a bunch of guys playin' ball in a field.
Baseball is and should not be just about numbers;
there are intangibles that cannot be quantified yet
should still be acknowledged and rewarded.

Considering his position, size, and era, McAuliffe
stacks up well among historically strong-hitting

Tigers. McAuliffe was nothing if not flexible throwing left but swinging right, playing all sorts of positions, and doing a smooth transition from All-Star shortstop to MVP-caliber second baseman. Rare among infielders of the day, McAuliffe was in the all-time top ten in five offensive categories when he retired. He was nothing if not flexible, playing pitcher, shortstop, third base, second base, and was an unofficial batting coach and mentor to younger players. With all those different positions seemed to come an equal number of injuries; in 1965, he suffered a broken hand—and in '66, he was sick with food poisoning during the MLB All Star game. Most of all, he battled a bad knee injury that required surgery in July 1969, which knocked him out for remainder of the season. Some say that the knee was left over from the rough and tumble championship season the year before. Whatever the case, it was debilitating. But McAuliffe suffered in silence. It was always his way.

At the Tiger 'Old Timers' game in 1999 as the stadium was preparing to close, he was remembered fondly and often—something that touched his heart and made him a bit misty eyed according to folks there. As quoted by Tim Wendel in his book 'Summer of '68', "Dick McAuliffe was the kind of player you could always count on, and you know he will have your back. It's hard to picture that '68 team without him." Participating in the closing ceremonies at Tiger Stadium in 1999

was special for him. "Being there again was
wonderful but you hated to see such a great
stadium be retired. But you know, life has to go
on," McAuliffe said. "To me there was nothing like
Tiger Stadium, and those devoted Detroit fans!"
Fond memories.

Towards the end of his life McAuliffe shared his
thoughts on the modern business of baseball. He
did not like the fact that fans had to basically
mortgage their homes to be able to afford a ticket
to see a ball game! "I think there are too many
teams with watered down talent, some of whom
should be playing in Double A or Triple A! The
infield play is fine but the outfield play stinks.
These guys don't even know how to catch a ball
properly and get rid of it to make a play at the
plate," he explained. "Their body is not closed to
begin with and they wind up and take a couple of
crow hops before they throw. I follow the game a
little more now that the Tigers are successful
again. I think they're going to be real contenders
for the next several years," he added hopefully.

He knows of what he speaks. He retired among
Detroit's all-time top ten in five offensive
categories. And McAuliffe was among the
American League leaders in triples eight times,
and his ability to draw walks also increased his
offensive output, ending his career with a .343 on-
base percentage. In the 1980s, Bill James ranked
McAuliffe the 22nd all-time best second baseman

in his well regarded Historical Baseball Abstract.

McAuliffe was a lifetime .247 hitter, but that does not reflect his true value to his team; in 1968 he led the AL in runs scored despite hitting only .249. He did other important things well, like drawing walks and hitting for power (197 career home runs). He was among the better offensive infielders of the era. Jim Price, a backup catcher behind Bill Freehan for the '68 Tigers (and now a radio broadcaster for the team), told The Detroit Free Press upon McAuliffe's death, "We had a lot of fights back in those days, and 'Mad Dog' was always right there. Not mean at all, but you do him or his teammates wrong…they had to pay the price!" he said. And how does one ever put a value on that?

Sipping iced tea at a Florida golf course clubhouse years later looking back on his time at the plate, McAuliffe said sagely, "I played as hard as I could. I always thought I gave 100 percent, and was proud of the feats I

accomplished," he said. Always one to be hard on himself, he continued, "I thought overall...I should have done better. That's just my personal feeling. But I think I've been successful. I always played hard and was very determined, something I learned from my high school coach." Price, a past co-host of the Tiger radio broadcasts, recalled his teammate McAuliffe warmly following Dick's death. According to Price, McAuliffe was, "The best guy and the best teammate. He played hard every single day." True enough.

Every Tiger fan has a memory of Dick McAuliffe and for most it's either..."He's my favorite player," or "I always tried to copy his batting style!" He is one of the most popular Tigers in online forums yet the powers that be in Cooperstown and the sports writers across the USA, who vote on who gets inducted, have so far gotten it wrong.

The National Baseball Hall of Fame Museum in Cooperstown, New York is operated by private interests. It serves as the repository of the history of baseball in the United States and displays baseball-related artifacts and exhibits, honoring those who have excelled in playing, managing, and serving the sport. The Hall's motto is "Preserving History, Honoring Excellence, Connecting Generations." If that is the case, in this author's opinion, McAuliffe should have a plaque there.

Membership in the Major League Baseball Hall of Fame should require more than just good HR and RBI numbers. How do you put a valuation on players like him who put butts in the seats? Among his achievements most do not know that Dick McAuliffe tied the Major League record by going the entire 1968 season without grounding into a single double play and at the time he was the only American League player to ever have done so.

To date, 13 Tigers have been inducted to the Baseball Hall of Fame in Cooperstown, New York

—and many players with lesser stats have been inducted. Amazingly in a severe case of oversight Dick McAuliffe has yet to be inducted. He was close in the 1981 voting when he came in approximately 35th. Here's hoping that error will be corrected in the very near future. How about this? Let the fans vote. He'd get in on the first round! Here's hoping that this oversight will be rectified, and that Mrs. McAuliffe can see her husband inducted into the Hall.

It is rare, especially today, to see someone that is almost predestined to become spectacular but we do see it…like a young prodigy making wonderful music at the age of 9 or achieving a perfect score in gymnastics as a teenager or painting a masterpiece at 10 years old. But that was the young man from the countryside of Connecticut. The game was his destiny and his life. Through the ups and downs of Major League Baseball, he was living proof that someone with basic talents who makes maximum use of them will always be further ahead than others who take their natural God given talents for granted.

From his very first minor league pitch with the Erie Sailors, where he found professional pitching a challenge, to three All Star games and 14 successful seasons, Dick McAuliffe was where God and the universe meant for him to be.

According to Sports Illustrated Magazine, 1968

was "Year of the
Pitcher" with Tiger
Denny McLain
winning 31 games—
but there were many
other stories unfolding,
that season with some
of the most iconic
games in history being
played. Mickey Mantle
in the east and Willie
Mays in the west
dominating the
headlines, it was no
wonder the Tigers
always seemed to get
below-the-fold
coverage from the
media of the day, and that was especially true for
McAuliffe who did not cater to the media at all.

Into that season strode what some consider
baseball's last true champions of the golden era:
the scrappy, come-from-behind, never-say-die
Detroit Tigers, who captured their first American
League pennant since Second World War and then
proceeded to rally from a three games to one
deficit in the World Series to upset the heavily
favored champion St Louis Cardinals. The boys
from the Motor City went the full distance and
came out victorious.

He was a young man that stepped into the maelstrom of professional baseball as a handsome, cocky, muscular, Irish-Italian with one of the strangest batting stances in the history of the game and the cumulation of which was McAuliffe's beloved statue and successful career. But it is his performance in the dynamic series of '68 that's etched into almost every fan's memory. For those of us who lived and died with the Tigers of the 1960s, listening to the legendary voice of the Tigers Ernie Harwell on a simple transistor radio… we will never forget the special man that was Champion Dick "Mad Dog' McAuliffe!

A Connecticut Treasure
A Fan Persective

Michael Hayden grew up as a baseball obsessed young boy in suburban Connecticut of the 1950's and 60's. "I was always thinking about the next time I could take the field or about major league ballplayers, their stats and lives filled my every waking minute. I wanted to be one of them!" he said. The idea of being able to play every day and make a living competing on the highest level was a dream to him and most young men.

"Imaging traveling to and playing in the iconic historic ballparks of the day!" he said. "Of course I had my favorite players and foremost of these was Detroit Tiger and Boston Red Sox player Dick McAuliffe. I soaked up all the information I could find about him; newspapers, sports magazines, baseball history and bios from the library. Ballgames were mostly listened to on the radio, but I watched a game or two on our small black and white TV on the weekends," he shared.

Connecticut is very rich in sports history. But in those days there were few high school players in Hayden's area being signed to play pro ball. "I started hearing about someone from Connecticut on the Detroit Tigers," Hayden said. "So I was on a mission to find out all I could. Dick McAuliffe was not only from Connecticut, he was from a town less than 20 miles from me! He personified all the

hopes and dreams I and so many of my friends
had." Hayden followed his career all the way
through to his time with the Red Sox, and as
manager of the Bristol (Connecticut) Red Sox farm
team in the 1970s.

Many years later Hayden met Dick's daughter
Mary at an optical store where they both worked.
They had a lot in common, became good friends.

Dick returns to Farmington, CT after winning the 1968 World Series.
(He's in the center in a black suit)

"One day in early fall, Mary McAuliffe asked me
if I would like to go with her and her family to a
World Series game at Fenway Park in Boston," he
said. "It was game three of the Sox vs Mets. Not
only were my Red Sox in the 1986 World Series

99

but I'm actually going to the game!" he said. "Not only that but I was going with one of my all-time favorite ballplayers!"

It was a dream day for Hayden "I met Mary, her Dad, and her Mom, Joanne, and together we drove to Boston. They were very friendly and warm and put me right at ease. At Fenway, Dick pointed out a few areas on the field where balls would be hit, or oddities and events that took place in games he had played there." It was a pro-level play by play!

During the game, McAuliffe was very patient as Hayden asked many questions about strategies, situational baseball and what the players might be thinking. It was awesome. "Getting this firsthand knowledge was golden, a dream, and the memory of a lifetime," said Hayden.

Over the years many major league ballplayers have spoken at The World Series Club of Hartford County, CT. where Hayden is a long time member. Chartered in 1926, the club brings in present and former baseball luminaries for a dinner, speech, autographs and Q&A. "There were a few former teammates of Dick that spoke there, like Denny McLain who spoke very highly of Dick. He was revered as a teammate and everyone who knows him says he is such a gentleman, he said. McAuliffe had been a speaker there a few times and entertaining the crowds with funny and intriguing stories.

"I am proud to have known Dick McAuliffe. He was a kind, generous, friendly, unpretentious gentleman," said the fan who now is retired and living in Connecticut with his wife and # kids. "Dick McAuliffe was my favorite player of all time! He worked hard to get to and stay in the major leagues for 16 years. His perseverance was an inspiration to me and so many others. He was an all-star both on and off the field. He is indeed a Connecticut treasure!"

Michael Hayden is a lifelong Baseball fan, professional musician, and retired music teacher. He lives with his wife Cathy in South Windsor, CT.

It's been a long, long time . . .

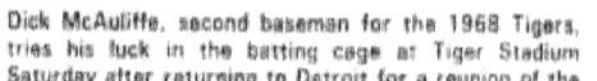

Dick McAuliffe, second baseman for the 1968 Tigers, tries his luck in the batting cage at Tiger Stadium Saturday after returning to Detroit for a reunion of the World Championship team. Mac hasn't played big league ball since 1975, but even though he was a little rusty he obviously enjoyed himself.

Chapter 9

Stats, Clips and Pics… oh my!

McAuliffe to Manage
NEW ORLEANS, Dec. 3 (AP)—Dick McAuliffe, an infielder who retired at the end of last season, was named today manager of Bristol, the Boston Red Sox farm club in the Eastern League. McAuliffe, 35 years old, spent last season with the Red Sox after 13 years with Detroit.

BASEBALL ALMANAC

Year	Age	Team	G	AB	R	H	2B	3B	HR	GRSL	RBI	BB	IBB	SO	SH	SF
1960	21	Tigers	8	27	2	7	0	1	0	0	1	2	0	6	0	0
1961	22	Tigers	80	285	36	73	12	4	6	0	33	24	0	39	1	1
1962	23	Tigers	139	471	50	124	20	5	12	0	63	64	3	76	0	4
1963	24	Tigers	150	568	77	149	18	6	13	1	61	64	1	75	7	5
1964	25	Tigers	162	557	85	134	18	7	24	1	66	77	8	96	5	3
1965	26	Tigers	113	404	61	105	13	6	15	0	54	49	4	62	0	1
1966	27	Tigers	124	430	83	118	16	8	23	1	56	66	2	80	4	3
1967	28	Tigers	153	557	92	133	16	7	22	1	65	105	4	118	2	4
1968	29	Tigers	151	570	95	142	24	10	16	0	56	82	8	99	1	3
1969	30	Tigers	74	271	49	71	10	5	11	0	33	47	1	41	1	2
1970	31	Tigers	146	530	73	124	21	1	12	1	50	101	7	62	3	2
1971	32	Tigers	128	477	67	99	16	6	18	0	57	53	4	67	1	1
1972	33	Tigers	122	408	47	98	16	3	8	0	30	59	7	59	1	0
1973	34	Tigers	106	343	39	94	18	1	12	2	47	49	5	52	2	0
1974	35	Red Sox	100	272	32	57	13	1	5	0	24	39	5	40	3	1
1975	36	Red Sox	7	15	0	2	0	0	0	0	1	1	0	2	1	0

Career		G	AB	R	H	2B	3B	HR	GRSL	RBI	BB	IBB	SO	SH	SF
16 Years		1,763	6,185	888	1,530	231	71	197	7	697	882	59	974	32	30

Team	Baserunning Statistics			Other Positions			Common Hitting Ratios		
	SB	CS	SB%	PH	PR	DH	AB/HR	AB/K	AB/RBI
1960 Tigers	0	0	.000	1	0	n/a	0.0	4.5	27.0
1961 Tigers	2	3	.400	8	0	n/a	47.5	7.3	8.6
1962 Tigers	4	2	.667	10	0	n/a	39.3	6.2	7.5
1963 Tigers	11	5	.688	2	0	n/a	43.7	7.6	9.3
1964 Tigers	8	5	.615	2	0	n/a	23.2	5.8	8.4
1965 Tigers	6	9	.400	3	0	n/a	26.9	6.5	7.5
1966 Tigers	5	7	.417	11	1	n/a	18.7	5.4	7.7
1967 Tigers	6	5	.545	2	0	n/a	25.3	4.7	8.6
1968 Tigers	8	7	.533	3	1	n/a	35.6	5.8	10.2
1969 Tigers	2	5	.286	2	0	n/a	24.6	6.6	8.2
1970 Tigers	5	6	.455	12	1	n/a	44.2	8.5	10.6
1971 Tigers	4	1	.800	8	0	n/a	26.5	7.1	8.4
1972 Tigers	0	0	.000	8	1	n/a	51.0	6.9	13.6
1973 Tigers	0	4	.000	7	2	1	28.6	6.6	7.3
1974 Red Sox	2	0	1.000	15	4	3	54.4	6.8	11.3
1975 Red Sox	0	0	.000	0	0	0	0.0	7.5	15.0

Career	SB	CS	SB%	PH	PR	DH	AB/HR	AB/K	AB/RBI
16 Years	63	59	.516	94	10	4	31.4	6.4	8.9

STATS
Dick McAuliffe

Full Name: Richard John McAuliffe
Nickname: 'Mad Dog'
Positions: Second Baseman, Shortstop and Third Baseman
Bats: Left / Throws: Right
5' 11", 176 lbs
Born: November 29, 1939, Hartford, CT
Died: May 13, 2016 (Aged 76), Farmington, CT
High School: Farmington High School, CT
Debut: September 17, 1960 (Age 20)
Last Game: September 1, 1975 (Age 35)
13 Seasons with the Detroit Tigers
3-time American League All-Star (1965-1967)
AL Runs Scored Leader (1968)
20-Home Run Seasons: 1964, 1966 & 1967
Won MLB World Series, Detroit Tigers, 1968

Career:
1,530 Hits
197 Home Runs
247 Batting Avg. Lifetime
696 Runs Batted In
1,763 career regular season games
Inducted Michigan Sports Hall of Fame 1986
Gold Key, Connecticut Sports Writers' Alliance, 1974
Connecticut High School Coaches Association Hall of Fame, 1984

Television Appearances (Actor)
•The Legend of Lylah Clare
Press Party Guest (uncredited), 1967

•A Guide for the Married Man
Man in Tennis Club Locker Room (uncredited), 1970

SUNNY

METRO
Stocks Lose
Trading Heavy
See Page 10, Section B

Detroit Free Press
ON GUARD FOR 137 YEARS

Vol. 138—No. 159 · Friday, October 11, 1968 · Ten Cents

! WE WIN !

City Goes Wild After Tiger Victory

BY BARBARA STANTON

Detroit went hell-bent for a hangover Thursday night in riotous, rowdy triumph after the Tigers won the World Series.

World champions!

At 4:06 p.m., Bill Freehan caught a pop fly in St. Louis and Detroit exploded like a magnificent firecracker.

AND A TROPHY TO PROVE IT: Exuberant Dick McAuliffe, left, with Jim Northrup, center, and Mickey Stanley hold it all as they display the trophy that goes to baseball's World Champions.

Tigers Avoid Welcoming Mob

The Big Victory

George Cantor's story of the Tigers' triumph. Page 1D.

Dick Mayer's World Series. Page 1A.

Violence and vandalism mar Tiger celebration. Page 4B.

Mickey Lolich's mother has "never worried about him—even today." Page 1C.

"It's my fault . . . I misjudged Northrup's hit"—Curt Flood. Page 2D.

"I'll never forget it"—Al Kaline. Page 3D.

More pictures on Page 11C and Back Page.

The Champions Weep in Joy

BY BOB TALBERT
Free Press Columnist

Quiz

1) What other sports did Dick play?

2) The Stadium was called what when built?

3) What happened in the late 50's that postponed Dick from joining the Tigers?

4) How many children did Dick have.

5) What is Tiger Stadium capacity?

6) For the incident with Tommy Johns how long was Dick suspended and how much was the MLB fine?

7) How many times did Dick make the MLB All Star team?

8) What was his most important attribute?

9) Besides Baseball what was Dick's favorite Sport?

10) What did Dick do when he retired?

Quiz Answers

1) Basketball, Football

2) Navin Field

3) Local Flood in CT.

4) 2, a girl and a boy

5) Approximately 53,000

6) Five days and $500

7) Three

8) Perseverance

9) Golf

10) Taught Baseball and had a Laundry Business

<u>LEARNING RESOURCES</u>

<u>Newspapers & Magazines</u>

Doyle, Al, "Tommy John: The Game I'll Never Forget, " Baseball Digest, May 2004.

Gammons, Peter, "McAuliffe Back as Bosox Lose Rico, " The Sporting News, September 6, 1975.

Green, Jerry, "Time Hasn't Taken Fight Out of Tigers Franchise," Detroit News, August 20, 2001.

Hawkins, Jim, "Tigers Tabbing Oglivie as a Regular," The Sporting News, December 13, 1975, 50.

"Majors Fear Loss of Players From a Possible Military Draft," New York Times, July 23, 1961, S2.

Murray, Jim, "Sticks to Riches," Los Angeles Times, June 9, 1965, B1.

O'Gara, Roger, "Eastern's Openers Hit Fouls in Bad Weather," The Sporting News, May 3, 1975.

"Ryan Hurls His 2nd No-Hitter of Year," New York Times, July 16, 1973, 37.

Spoelstra, Watson, "Kaline Marks 27th Birthday," The Sporting News, January 3, 1962.

"Tigers Buy McAuliffe," New York Times, September 16, 1960, C2.

LEARNING RESOURCES-2

Books

James, Bill, The New Bill James Historical Abstract (New York: Free Press, 2001), 497-8.

Johnson, Lloyd, and Miles Wolff, eds., The Encyclopedia of Minor League Baseball, 2nd ed., (Durham, North Carolina: Baseball America, 1997).

McConnell, Bob, and David Vincent, eds., SABR Home Run Encyclopedia (New York: Macmillan, 1996).

Stern, Chris, Where Have They Gone? (New York: Tempo Books, 1979), pg. 118

Smith, Brad, 'A History of Detroit Tigers Shortstops' January, 1999

FACEBOOK FAN PAGES

The Official Detroit Tigers Group
Detroit Tigers True Fans
Detroit Tiger Talk.
Detroit Tigers 1968 World Series Champions
Fans of the 1968 World Series Champion
Detroit Tigers
Mad Dog Detroit Tiger Dick McAuliffe

<u>Acknowledgments</u>

The Detroit Tigers
The Estate of Dick McAuliffe
Major League Baseball
City of Detroit Public Affairs
The Detroit Free Press
The Detroit News
WJR-AM
The Sharon Harvill Foundation
The McAuliffe Heritage Center
Journalist Jerry Green
Photographer Mike McCormick
Photographer Fred Scherman
Photographer Paul Tepley
Associated Press Images
USA Today Sports Images
Alzheimer's Foundation of America
Kimberly Ball
Chris Bockelman
Mary & JP Boyle
Eve Ifft
Michael Hayden
John Gildersleeve
Topps Trading Card Co.
Sports Pictures USA

<u>Special Thanks to:</u>
The Society for American Baseball Research
at Arizona State University

The Baseball Almanac.com

NUTS!
The Life & Times of General Tony McAuliffe
Tom McAuliffe
From the Award Winning Author of "Mr. Mulligan"
Volume 4: The McAuliffe Series
Detroit Tiger Dick McAuliffe
MAD DOG
TOM MCAULIFFE
AMAZON / KINDLE &
WWW.AUTHORTOMMCAULIFFE.COM
MR. MULLIGAN
The Life of Champion Armless Golfer Tommy McAuliffe
Tom Patrick McAuliffe II
FROM THE AWARD WINNING AUTHOR OF "MR. MULLIGAN"...
NUMBER 3 IN "THE MCAULIFFE SERIES"
TEACHER ASTRONAUT CHRISTA MCAULIFFE
THROTTLE UP!
TOM MCAULIFFE

Books by
Tom McAuliffe

• **Mr. Mulligan** - *The Life of Champion Armless Golfer Tommy McAuliffe*

• **NUTS!** - *The Life & Times of General Tony McAuliffe*

• **Throttle Up!** - *Teacher Astronaut Christa McAuliffe*

• **Mad Dog!** - *Detroit Tiger Dick McAuliffe*

• 2023 Autobiography

Available as Books, eBooks and Audiobooks!

Please visit:
WWW.AUTHORTOMMCAULIFFE.COM

Please leave us a Review!